First published in the UK by UniVerse Press

UniVerse Press is an imprint of Beacon Books and Media Ltd
Earl Business Centre, Dowry Street, Oldham OL8 2PF UK.

First edition published in 2022

www.beaconbooks.net

ISBN   978-1-915025-00-5   Paperback
ISBN   978-1-915025-01-2   Hardback
ISBN   978-1-915025-02-9   Ebook

Cataloging-in-Publication record for this book is available from the British
Library

Cover design by Raees Mahmood Khan

SINGULARITIES

PAUL MEIN

For my beautiful wife Angela, always so wise and patient.

Contents

I

II

III

IV

V

VI

I

High Broadwood I

Here and there, the flues have collapsed,
their umbilical ties severed.
Like a skeleton of a shark's jaw,
an arch is exposed to light, revealing
the well-constructed tunnel, surprisingly high.
There is no trace of boy here,
working, breathing in the life-shortening fumes,
a flickering light holding back
the weight of the dark.
Only a fern grows, in the sunshine
at the broken entrance,
like a plant of remembrance.
On the hill's brow, the stacks stand,
fingered to the sky, headstones for unnamed boys.

High Broadwood II

(a nineteenth-century lead mine in Allendale, Northumberland)

'For reasons of safety and the general good of the community, the Company proposes to site chimneys two and one half miles from the smelt site, connected by two flues constructed overground. By this method, noxious and harmful vapours will be dispersed away from human habitation.'

The people of Allendale felt this concern
for their health most deeply
when the fumes blew back to the town
on the westerly winds, as they often did.

The same sense of civic duty lay behind
the provision of education;
all ten year olds would read and write.
What waste.
These literate boys, equipped with tools
to broaden horizons, sent into
the constriction of a still-warm flue
with tools to scratch leadened detritus
from its walls and vaulted roof.
What waste.
Scrapings measured in thousands of pounds
for the owners, profit made
on the headaches, vomiting, numbness,
dementia and premature death
of the young workers.

Teacher – Timbuktu

Timbuktu was the seat of Islamic learning in the 16th. and 17th centuries. Fundamentalists and fanatics have tried to destroy irreplaceable manuscripts.

This is my lot. Dry, red sand
on a roof in a town at the edge of the world,
the walls low, overlooking the tents
in the courtyard below.

Here, barefoot on a woven mat,
time marked by the passage
of sun overhead, each shadow
a different minute,
I kneel with my students,
write with the hand of my ancestors.

In my family, there is a tale
of a time long gone,
when scholars exceeded locusts;
hard to believe now,
a scant half dozen
gathering to learn the ancient scripts,
showing a modicum of interest
in true heritage.

But in the land of sand-devils, scorching days,
nights the cold of space and stars,
if I can kindle the ember of curiosity,
nurture the flickering flame of interest,
these manuscripts, fragile, threatened,
dangerous for the truths they contain,
will be safe on a roof
in a town at the edge of the world.

In the eyes

Squatting in dusty heat,
cowering under words of hate,
two hundred lost hopes
peer from prisons of cloth,
appeal for help,
look for a father's smile,
a mother's understanding,
long for everyday comfort
in familiar things, the anchor
of people who hold them precious.

'Commodities,' the man rants;
'Bartering pieces.'
He rails against their right to learn,
to hold to their faith,
seeks to keep them in thrall
to his desolate ideology.
He is a man frightened
of the light in their eyes—
a weak man dangerous
in his fear.

On a wing and a prayer

Pavements and kerbstones,
the gaps between parked cars,
belong to sparrows and to us.
We share the dust and grit,
the filthy puddles from the water-cannon,
our children swaddled to us
against the hard shock of concrete;
we live in litter, the scatter of plastic bottles,
bags splattered against razor-wire
like emptied jelly-fish,
stubs of angry cigarettes,
sweat, reek of hurried bodies,
harried from one brief respite to another
on the road to some kind of freedom.
It's a matter of degree—
gun fire and bombs to unexploded mines,
poison gas to tear gas,
one hate-filled law to the next.
Borders close and open on us;
like Skinner's rats we work out a route
then replan, desperate for the reward of safety.

The sparrows can fly.

Out of sight

See her   that girl   over there
the waitress who moves
like a princess from the Arabian Nights.

Find in the eyes
of this young woman
some hopeful future from a past...

of faces without hope
grimed-white as bandage rags
dust that ghost-shrouds everything
devilling behind battered Toyota trucks
full of excitable boys with rifles for toys
blood on the fluttering pages of a holy book
a woman rocking a pram filled with a memory
row on row of tents flapping
sails on a wasteland   castaways in dogma...

Look through her eyes
at what she hides there
then tell her she has to return.

Aleppo

A fragrant mowing on the last
warm day of summer,
or the first of autumn;
the big trees across the river
not browned yet, oak and chestnut
still sprightly in the stiffening breeze.

I pause, sweaty from the cutting,
relieved that for a few months
I'll be spared this chore,
but the grass springs back,
hopeful of another trimming
before the frosts.

Coffee steams where my wife
left it, on the table
under the sap-sticky lime tree;
I sit, try to take in the still-lush view, enjoy
the children's laugh and squabble
but I am nagged by—

an image, culled from newsreels—
a man sits at a wonky table
in a shattered street,
full of house-shaped holes, silences, ash—

ash covers everywhere;
the man could be anyone, any race.
He is cloaked grey
with humanity's inhumanity.

He sits on a twisted plastic chair
at the wonky table, a cup with no handles
in front of him and   a chess board on which
it is difficult to distinguish black and white.

Peering over a wall, standing against all odds,
a muted splash of colour—
a small tree, a fig perhaps,
luminous.

The man stands; he hasn't touched
his cup or chess pieces.
Shackled by his world, he shuffles
past the tree—and stops.

He reaches to its greenness,
as if to say...   as if he's thinking...

The truth is, I can't know
what thoughts or feelings charge
his wire-thin, trauma-shaped body.
I haven't been where he has, he is,
the spoilage of his life
reflected in his shoulders' stoop,
the shadows in his eyes.
I can only dimly guess at
the lead weight of his loss.
I know I could not walk
even a yard in his lonely shoes,
in his monochrome uncertainty.

The tree moves in the breeze,
a branch touches my shoulder.
I am grateful for small aches and pains,
for a verdant present.

Ready

from 'Behind every hero' collection

Smoke rises like prayers
from the dying night-fires
of the last of the army.
After the longest siege,
the muted words are of
the blood lust rage of Achilles,
deaths of heroes and companions
slaked in dust and chariot horse trample,

home,
wives,
children,
lovers.

The last few calls of odds at dice;
intended sacrifices end up
in men's bellies, appeasing hunger
rather than sacred sensibilities.

In the creeping pre-dawn light
Odysseus watches the horse—
huge, heavy with warriors,
the creation of his cunning—
trundle to the plain
before the metropolis;
sees the first rays glint
on the wall-guards' spears,
senses their curiosity
about this equine apparition,
emerging from early mists.

He envisages the city's sack,
readies himself for the voyage beyond.

Garden, September 1914

Overnight, an R in the month,
dew-damp underfoot,
the smell of cut grass hovering,
the last mow of the season.

Smiles of cosmos
and rudbeckia cheer up
tired hostas,
fading, lilac-green hydrangea.

Commas, tortoiseshells, peacocks,
busy two warm days ago, have vanished,
leaving wind-waving gaura empty,
browning buddleia deserted.

The garden's readying for change—
a dustiness on tired trees,
wasps dying-summer drunk,
an earliness of last light;

a train hoots, distant,
from the space left by sunset.
Under the vicarage eaves fourteen nests,
quiet, emptied for a season.

Swallows muster for a leaving
as young men soon will,
innocent in the shortening days.

Night time manoeuvres

After the dry heat of the day,
cooler. Musicians – accordion,
fiddle, guitar – tuned up
under pin-cushion stars;
in shirt sleeves, skirts, blouses,
townsfolk filled long trestles,
poured wine made ruby
in the light from hurricane lamps;
smoke from Gauloise, Gitane, Disque Bleu
swirled through warm cadences
of strangers' voices; children
raced, chased, unchecked,
safe in familiar shadows.

Meat seared, spat, sizzled,
flames sputtered, soared,
plates filled, emptied,
glasses replenished.
Music started, couples
moved onto the beaten-earth floor,
little ones waltzed by grandmas.
With a dearth of young men,
grim-faced older sisters two-stepped
brothers, all elbows and knees.
The girl, dark, hair crimson-ribbon wrapped
took my hand in her thin,
strong fingers. 'Dansez.'
I followed her smile to the dancing place.

Through her meagre dress
I felt the bones of her shoulders,
barely fleshed. I had never
held a girl like that before.
My first taste of wine,

plum, blackberry, lent my mouth
an eloquence, my feet
a grace; we danced without moving.
I asked her name. 'Votre nom?'
'Clothilde.' I could not tell her mine;
she stole my breath with hers;
she tasted – smelt– of cherry,
damson, garlic, raw onion;
of loam and endless skies.

I loved her instantly, for ever,
as long as the kiss lasted,
until she was clucked away
by a moustached matron in black,
who "looked at me daggers,"
as ma would have it.
Clothilde turned, fired me
with her eyes. I had never seen
or touched a more beautiful thing;
I loved her even more
in her disappearing.
More wine later, by the
brass-button gleaming flames,
my pals bantered—

'You've clicked; you've scored;
when's the wedding?'
Jimmy began to sing,
"Madamoiselle from Armentieres."
'Best friends ever,' I wanted to say;
instead, a slowrising bubble,
glorious red wine gushed,
lost over boots and soil.

Jimmy shook me out of sleep.
'The girl left this for you.'
a ribbon, blood red.

I looked about; only
the pals remained. Leaving behind
the best night I ever had,

we stumbled back
along muddied tracks
to rising larks,
the morning's first shells.

Sunday by the sea – 1952

Ice cream, candy floss, fish and chips,
twenty Players and a pint of Ex.,
knotted hanky hat against the sun,
rolled up trousers, pallid legs.
A paddle and a kick about,
snooze and sunburn, time for a tea;
deck chair watch over sandcastle bairns,
fifties Sunday down by the sea.

From nowhere, no warning, he spoils it all—
too much ale, sun, sand; above all, too much sand;
he's seen and had enough of that.
Five years in a place, a war in which he had
no choice, no wife, no child.
All that pointless time in irritant sand,
nostril filling, eyeball scratching, food gritting
ever present sand.

He never again wants to see it
or feel it abrasive
against the desert legacy
of his skin scurf psoriasis.

His uproar upsets the little ones,
who scuttle, like hermit crabs,
under protective skirts
of silence-shocked mothers.
His wife reaches to him,
wanting to wrap up his hurt in her arms,
toss it to the uncaring breeze,
but he is in a different place,
with his mind's dead, his desert army pals.
The other fathers play their parts,
guide him to the pub on the hill—

they know that wounds suppressed inside
are compelled to surface somewhere,
like stems of kelp, root-wrenched
from secure anchoring
by deep sea surge, shore shattering waves.

A fifties Sunday by the sea,
flensed by distant sands.

Airman

He flicks his cigarette,
sparks bouncing
from the pavement's shadows;

hearing his name, he turns,
smiling for her camera,
angling his airman's cap.

Between this photo and the next,
he will look from his gunner's place
on fireblooms in cities.

I look like him,
the man in the crumpled picture,
the man with far-seeing eyes.

They never spoke of him,
my dad, my other uncle,
their younger brother.

There was a lady I saw only once,
when I was three or four,
from behind my mother's skirts.

His fiancée, I was told;
she was tall
and reached to touch my face.

I look like him;
I never met him;
I am blood-tied to his ghost.

On this September morning,
the wind dying,
I am held by his grave marker.

Marks on a mountain, lives on a monument

Raw the day. Sere.

Fresh from snows on Brizzle Crags,
gusts race, maul down the valley,
whip gorse and broom,
bend broad-leaved trees,
chase clouds.
In the fold and crease of
law and tor, tracked
to long-forgotten places,
the wind seeks out weakness,
scours and stupefies face and mind.

The dry stone wall,
circular, like a sheep stell,
diverts the wind's bite.
Here is shelter for walkers
and memories, chiselled and cast
in granite and bronze,
the black, polished block
dedicated to airmen of
different countries,
different sides,
different times,
who lost their lives in misted Cheviots.

Behind the slab,
like an aeroplane wing,
the Roll of Honour—
Irving, MacDonald,
Sokolinsky, O'Kane,
Schulz, Freyh-
fifty seven names in all.
They are surrounded, protected

by their planes, incised
in perpetual flight over
the stylised, curlew hills;
beyond this final flight,
real hills reveal, then hide,
made invisible by the lour of cloud.
Here, in the company of other men,
long gone from the Borders,
within the sound of College Burn,
"Duty Done - They Sleep."

A custom of long standing

Pant – a communal water tap

In the Britain of swinging sixties,
she drove her pony and trap
as she had done since the Great War,
to the market town five miles away.
Every morning, this doughty woman of Tynedale
with the blood of Romans, Scots,
Thracians, Vikings, Saxons and Normans
alchemical in her veins,
disdained the elements or rejoiced in them,
trotted on for bread and gossip,
meeting at the old pant, to satisfy a thirst
for companionship and confidences.

On some gentle mornings, the mist weakly banished
from the river's valley by a sun
worn out with its efforts to warm,
she would stand, peaceful in herself, near the ruins,
on the same spot where, as a young bride,
she waited for word from the Front.
Her handbag held three things,
there for decades; a photograph,
a couple, smiling, sepia'd, in uniform
and wedding dress; a silver Roman coin,
halved, inscriptions illegible; a letter,
learnt by heart, folded, brittle by years—
"My darling wife, How I thrill to those words..."

She listened to voices only she heard,
as buzzards mewed over long-settled, untamed land.

II

Reiver daughter

*Reivers were raiders across the English-Scottish borders in the 14th.
to 16th. centuries*

She's a daughter of Border Reivers,
no quarter asked for or given.
Steel grey bun fierce drawn back
from a once youthful face with cheekbones carved
from the Whin Sill and a steady, deep gaze
that marks out sinner from sinned.

Red raw hands that have milked a thousand cows,
scrubbed floors and clothes, brewed beer,
are swollen knuckled, veined like drovers' roads—
as quick with a gully in slice and slash
as any man's, to protect bairns,
guard the cattle. In a world full of turmoil,
midnight burnings, taking vengeance is as
natural as baking bread.

A hard woman for cruel times.

Yet, when a little one rests, in its cot,
or the summer swallows
return to their under eave nests, she smiles,
the world stops for a brief breath time,
lightens its warring face
and shares with her an easier place.

Margaret Stothard

from the radio play 'The Witch of Edlingham'

Early morning's a joy.

The time of softlight,
when beasts low gentle as I pass
and birds call from perch to perch,
not yet ready to move to the day.
The last of night things
creep, crawl, swoop, scuttle
to their lairs and hides
to sleep away sunlight.

Some folk, if they're up,
emptyin' theirsels of last night's ale,
think aam one of the night waalkers,
caal is for it, but them that knaas is
knaas different.

Aa luv the dew, damp between me toes;
ofttimes, aa wash me face in it,
it's that sweet and smooth.
Ye want to try it hinny.
They say if ye rinse yer eyes with dew
afore the sun comes up on the first day of spring,
it'll help ye see clearer
the man ye're to marry.
Some of yis need
as much help as ye can get.

A flask of dew aalways helps
with the making' of simples an' aal.
That's why folk come to me ye knaa;
for a cure for what ails them—

mistletoe, thistle, chestnut, henbane,
hawthorn, foxglove, feverfew, dandelion
and more.
The plants aa gather. My plants.
Safe in proper use,
dangerous in the wrang hands.

Some come in the day,
when there's nae shame in what they seek—
to bring a bairn's fever doon,
to settle upset bellies,
to bind a wound, mek it whole,
to disappear warts and wens.

After dark, it's different.
A soft knock on the door,
shiftin' sideways glances,
the shawl coverin' the face—
as if anybody waadn't know
who they were.
These are whisperin' visits,
the "Aa knaa a girl, a friend,
who needs help" visits
the "Aa knaa a man, a friend,
who canna perform his husbandly duties
as he should" visits.

Aa dae what aa can; they'll often pay
with a rabbit or wood for the fire.
Folk are grateful for
what aa dae for them.

But aa draw the line—
"Hoo can aa mek coos hev the staggers?"
"Hoo can aa mek land barren?"
"Hoo can aa get shot of the man
who's mekin' me life a misery?"-

because aa knaa these are dark things.
Secrets.
And when aa say no,
people divn't like it.
They caal is...

witch

      witch

          WITCH

Betty of Whitwell

*In the 1980s, during quarrying, a burial monument dating from
3800/3900 B.C. was uncovered. In addition to containing de-
fleshed bones of several individuals, a separate burial chamber
was discovered, containing the complete skeleton of a girl with
arrowheads strategically placed around the body. For the time, this
separate, single burial was unique. The girl was named Betty by
archaeologists.*

I saw her. Betty.
Betty in a box,
a plain grey box,
cardboard, stored
with other 'artefacts'
on dexion shelving.

The woman revered
as sage/seer/sacrifice
irreverently taken from
her interment site,
sleeping the aeons alone,
closed off from the ordinary,
the flensed, who held
their tumbled bones in common,
ready for the god of flight
to visit, arrow her away
through the tomb's portal
to be reborn in her rightful place,
welcomed by stars.

Three years later,
I asked for Betty again.
She was missing— gone,
no-one knew where,
'misplaced' in a bureaucratic mess.
Did she escape to the heavens after all,
through the speculations of experts,
the gaps in their knowledge?

Grace

*Grace Darling became famous for her part in the rescue of survivors
from the Forfarshire, shipwrecked off the Farne Islands in 1838.
She died, aged 26, in 1842. Her brother became the first lighthouse
keeper on Coquet Island, just before her death.*

South of the Fabled Farnes
the island reaches out fingers of rock
to its better known cousins,
last outcrops of the Great Whin Sill.
From his lighthouse eyrie
a brother seeks out his sister
on the northern wild water of his memory.
Terns and seals,
wave and wind,
swap tales of
holy men and hermits, storms and shoals,
stories of her bravery,
while the light slices the darkness,
searches blindly
for her presence in the tumult.

The Fates see Penelope

from 'Behind every hero' collection

She stands by wave-slapped harbour rocks.
She looks to where sea and sky melt as one.
She waits for the return of a man long gone.

Her husband.

A trickster, a boaster,
a planner, a schemer.
Delayed from the long-over war.

But still, her husband.

Why does he not rush to her side
lusting to hold her take her to his bed
like a young bride after all this time?

Poseidon has intervened
caught up the man's life
in storm and seaweed twists.

That's why she weeps.

He is in Charon's shadow
held in balance
between sea and Styx.

We'll stay in her vigil a while.

Tarn (Beatrix's place)

Goose song on mercuried water,
skim of wings swooping
close to liquid hills.
Trace a vagabond breeze
ruffling the surface,
abstracts in brown, green, blue,
patterned by duck vees
and fish circles.

A snow-mountained distance
backdrops the quiet.

A hundred years ago a woman
walked this same ground,
saw rabbits in trousers
and ducks in bonnets.

Mermaid

I

Sea, sky as one,
Mother Carey's chickens and herring gull
chase across shag-skimmed waves.

Fishermen have long since shaken heads,
shoaled in their pub by the harbour,
reinforcing the wisdom of not putting out
in this weather, remembering those who once did
and never returned.
Attuned to weather,
they know the power of that east wind
blasting from Moscow to Craster
with nothing to absorb or give it pause between;
they fasten waterproofs, tug down woollen hats,
drain glasses and head out,
heads down, for home and fire.

The woman, buffeted at the end of the quayside,
is ill-equipped for the freezing fury around her;
the thin mac, pale blue, more suited to a spring stroll,
thin soled shoes and seaweeded hair entirely soaked.

She faces out, away from the ill-tempered calm in the harbour,
where boats struggle against restraining, bow-lined rope,
scraping against old, rough-hewn blocks; sea bears
seeking relief from salt water's itch.
Her ungloved hands are reddened, the finger tips,
holding the letter, whitening. She cries,
a necessary, insufficient description
of the outrage ravaging through her;
she is here because she can taste
the sea in her, can feel its
convulsive sympathy with her sobbing.

She rips the letter, sends scraps flying
with snow flakes, indistinguishable in their swirl.

Battling against itself the storm
rages, shakes—
a wave, higher than houses,
bullied to white topped fury
bursts over the harbour wall.
The woman is gone.

II

He hears the back door slamming
on its hinges, rimshots against
the night's bass thrum of

trees on the move, wind drummed,
thin, bare branches creating a sound
like the buffalo herds which took

a day or more to cross
the great American Midwest railway, in
prairie-shaking percussion.

Holding himself precious against the wind's tear,
he walks, muffled, into the dark,
seeking the rhythm of giants.

III

She wrote—

I left my world behind for you,
I gave up my privileges for you,
I suffered my father's ire
my mother's turning away.

For you.

For you, I swam out of my depth—

and sent it on the wind
with her crying.

IV

It's an uneasy start on the littoral,
early morning following the storm;
dunlins and oyster-catchers move nervously
in the shallows, untrusting of the great waters
still raging beyond them; clumps of deep sea ripped
brown slippery weed ropes pile up,
ready to stink if the sun should ever gain
the necessary heat. A battered seal
lies boneless on the sand, eyes already gone;
spin drifts of snow are caught on bleached wood sculptures;
the rudder and ribs of a jollyboat, 'NS1'
a fragment of its identity, are half-submerged
in a pool; in the distance, a flapping, light blue
movement, carried away by a wind which still has power.
This beach, on this morning, is no place to be at peace.

V

He startles from a sleep of buffalo dreams,
heat leaching from him as if he had been tight wrapped
in one of their coats; the quality of light
through thin curtains suggests a snow came
with last night's storm, a storm which makes him
thankful he has given up the sea, tied up with land.

He peers outside.
Hard digging today, but safer than waves
and unpredictable harvest from sea soil.

VI

Outside, stuck on his door, fragments of paper,
carried by the wind with the snowflakes,
inked letters taking on a tremor in the damp –

hind   *gave   leges*   *you*

ire   *away   dept*

he boils his kettle for breakfast tea, unaware
of the message carried to his house
in puzzled pieces.

For Grace, Marilyn, Diana...

Your everyday things—
objects of veneration, curiosity,
antiseptic behind glass,
missing the touch
that gave them meaning
in an ordinary life before
it became extraordinary;
your private possessions made public,
your unsuspecting soul bared
to the world's scrutiny.

Long-ago lady

(for Hilda's mam)

"Eeh I know your face,"
she said, the old woman
from twenty doors and sixty years away.

We sat, swapped tales for a while
as the tea grew tepid
as shadows swallowed the light.

Her shoulders, her voice, shed decades
as we coaxed from the black and white
albums of our mutual recollection
the back-to-back scrubbed step streets,
the chaos of higgle-piggle corner shops,
the school with its Victorian sternness,
prison playgrounds, open-air toilets and separate entrances,
names, faces and gossip of neighbours,
coloured them with our memories.

Perhaps too many reminders;
perhaps too many years— she tired,
her eagerness in thrall to age.

She made the same adjustments to scarf,
handbag, coat that my mother and aunty
used to, ready to meet the world.

"My daughter'll give you my address.
Call in any time for a cuppa.
We'll have another lovely chat."

She turned at the thresh, waved
with her free hand, the other linked firmly
into the crook of her daughter's elbow.

Say goodbye to the long-ago lady
I'd just met
I'd known forever.

Four women

(written as poet-in-residence at REACH, an organisation supporting adults with learning and other difficulties)

The circumstances of the mothers to whom I spoke were all different— each life a unique fingerprint. They had experienced, or in some cases, were still experiencing, challenges and difficulties above and beyond what is normally encountered in life. I didn't know what to expect when I met them, heard their stories.

The women talk— ordinary women
to whom extraordinary things had happened,
lives caught up with those of special people,
women making sense of the everyday
from the tangles of exceptionality.
Thoughts fleet across faces—
a memory of a smile, a set
of the head, a saying...

'*There were times, when he was beyond naughty, I used to take him and lock us both in the bathroom. I would sit on the toilet, singing, humming, until he calmed; my biggest threat was to put him under the cold shower. He didn't like that. People said you shouldn't, but you've got to find a way, a way to draw the boundaries. Difficult if he has no sense of limits.*'

'*His three brothers were "normal." They all played together. One day I saw some homework one of them had written for school—"My weekend" or some such thing. "We got up early on Sunday. Mum and dad were still asleep. We played Cowboys and Indians for ages. Me and J. and M. were Indians. We tied P. to the cot until breakfast..." Goodness knows what the teacher thought.*'

'When I saw the baby for the first time, I didn't hold out much hope. She was a baby who had multiple difficulties, who didn't feed. A ginger baby. At the limits. Floppy. Eyes closed. But then they opened briefly— and found mine.
With that one look, I knew we were going to be in it together, facing what
the world had to throw at us. Just that one look—a split second—a lifetime.'

'She didn't mix well at school, but her birthday was a big thing for her; everyone in the class would come with a present. I was at my wit's end one day because of her behaviour. The only thing I could think of to do was to cancel her birthday party.
On that morning, I was taking her out when, at the gate, all the mothers and children appeared with gifts. My daughter had written the invitations
herself. I felt I had to carry through my threat, so I told them there was to
be no party and why. Only one person phoned to support my decision.'

Careless words,
attitudes shaped in stereotypes,
fear of 'the other,'
the different;
ignorance, well-meaning wounding.

'I'll give him six months.'
'He'll need a wheelchair all his life.'
'You don't get attached to the handicapped ones, do you?'
'You're weird.'
'Why do they let them out amongst normal folk— it's not right.'
(at a queue for ice-cream).
'The looks, the whispers, the shaking of heads, the tut-tutting.'
'She can't help it can she—she's not right, poor thing.'
'I couldn't do what you do.'
'Mum did everything she could, but she was terrified for me; she carried the burden all her life.'

'For a long time, he denied anything was wrong with his son.'
'I didn't want respite for him—I wanted to look after my five-year-old.'
Accommodations—
we will all have to make them.
From this point on, nothing
will be the same;
each family link, knot and story
re-forged, re-tried, re-written
in shapes and patterns
unthought of, unexplored 'til now.
A kind of gravity
will keep us together,
the sharing of small triumphs
made heroic; the ordinary made special;
each person cherished.
Love, it's called.

*'The handicapped child is part of the family. The family is not
the child.'*
*'It's sometimes easy to overlook the needs of others in the family
because of the time and energy it takes to make arrangements
for one.'*
*'There's a balancing act to be done so that the rest of the family
get their fair share of things, of you.'*
*'It's an enhancing experience for other siblings. They learn about
caring, love, taking responsibility, in a very practical way.'*
'Sometimes there's a bit of resentment...'
'Yes, a sense of having favourites...'
'but there is in every family, isn't there?'
*'We didn't want him to be isolated—so we went on to have three
other kids.'*
*'Members of the family see "their" special person in a different way
from people outside the family. Despite my son's very obvious different
behaviour, his nephew described him as "My uncle M. You know,
the man with the hole in his hair."' (Referring to his bald patch).*
*'You think the family's going to be the best support, but often they're
dealing with their own grief, wondering why.'*

'It can put a strain on relationships. You've got to be able to sit down and talk things through without pulling your punches.'
'The greatest thing was having a strong husband for support. Without him, it would have been, not impossible, but very much more difficult.'
'You learn to pull together. It's vital. You develop different coping mechanisms, play off each other's strengths.'
'Sometimes it was like a tag team—I'd take over when my husband started to get frustrated, he'd come in when I was tired. Sometimes it was a united, exhausted front.'

Who writes the story of a life?
People brought together, uniquely,
for a sentence, a paragraph, a chapter,
crafting the sense of identity,
the personal integrity
the 'who am I?'
in clumsy or careful ways.

'You make constant efforts to be at the centre of services.
Although it's improving, you still find medical, social services, education, operating separately.'
'You assume someone will coordinate—but the onus is still with the family to make the running, what they need, when they need it.'
'Blown into a world you never thought of—contradictions, minefields, rages, frustration.'
'It's a difficult, fast learning curve, trying to quickly gain the expertise and energy you haven't got, to deal with organisations and individuals who frankly, aren't that helpful sometimes.'
'And all that while you're trying to met the 24/7 demands of your child, the rest of the family, life...'
'You learn fairly quickly to articulate your demands, find your way round the language to get at what you need; then you have to do it all over again
and again.'
'It's very easy to feel isolated. Finding a group like the old Westgate group
or REACH is wonderful.'

---

*'This sort of support is a lifeline. It really matters. People know what
you're going through instinctively...'
'and they'll help in practical ways...'
'Yes, so you don't have to start at the beginning. People are switched
on,
see what's required without you having to ask.'
'Everyone accepts your child for what he or she is; there's no labelling,
no limiting—just a belief in what they can achieve.'*

The balancing act
of seemingly impossible
spinning plates while
riding a bike,
pedalling, persevering.
A plate drops,
a pothole's hit,
equilibrium shatters,
an enervating darkness.
Look for glimmers,
pinpricks of light
in the blackout curtain,
pinpoints of hope,
the sunshine of people
who understand.
Back in the saddle,
stubbornly with stabilisers
wobble back
to the world outside.

*'You wear a mask for others. They need to see you being able to
cope, otherwise they think, "If she can't, how can I?"'
'It's the same with the children. They need to feel that you're the
stable, loving presence in their lives.'
'A lot of that is giving them the cues; looking for strategies that will
help them...*
*'And you. It's like a framework for your lives.'
'But the "mask," whatever it is, can't be false, otherwise it'll be seen*

through in a minute. You become the routines, masks, whatever.'
'We used to play cd's; it was a big part of our life together. M. loved
music, but I hardly put them on now he's gone.'
'You become very self-aware...how quite subtle changes in routine,

your attitude, your expressions, your voice have an effect, sometimes
out of all proportion...'
'It's all part of staying one step ahead...of trying to have a "normal"
life together.'

This is my precious,
my adored, whom I hope
the outside world will take
the time to get to know.

III

A Pascal

April. Lambsnowed fells.
A lark's skysong.
The burn in its shallow gully
burbling over pebbles.
A faint path's ending
by winter-vanishing woods.

Distant for a while from everyday blether,
steeped quiet in mysteries,
curious in my mind's world, I was persuaded
by a sleight of wild violets in a nearby copse,
a cuckoo feint through distant trees,
into a promised rising that Easter day.

Quiet places

St. Gregory the Great, Kirk Newton—the unique 12th century carving
of the Kilted Magi is to be found in this Northumberland church.

The cherry in blossom arches
over twelve headstones,
startlingly white, standing
to attention at the entrance
of the ancient churchyard
in this remote Cheviot place.

They share their rest
with legends on grey
lichened stones,
famous names, northern names
from Millfield, Doddington, Yeavering,
West and Kirk Newton.

These young men, boys
from the forties, fliers from
Canada, New Zealand,
made acquaintance with the hills,
exchanging their quiet
for the uproar of unexpected death.

The stream flows, enfolding;
blackbirds chase, chattering;
a skylark's song slips
through deep clouds;
Yeavering Bell, snow-haired, looks on;
Magi offer their gifts of peace.

Lindisfarne light

Dawn moves outside;
waders feed at water's edge,
a pair of ospreys fly high, catch the first rays,
watch to catch the day's first meal.

A cormorant swifts darkly
across the sea's chop;
gulls gather, raucous,
a run of herring beneath them.

Eadfrith, monk-turned-bishop
of the cold island priory
in the northern kingdom,
moves from the rose and copper awakening

into the candled dimness of the scriptorium,
considers his manuscript, wonders at the
weight of angels' wings, light as an
eider duck's feathers, strong as a sea-eagle's.

He thinks he has the right of them
on the incipit page for St. Matthew,
the angel lambent at his shoulder.
He hears the bell for prime,

walks to the chapel to lead the offices,
leaving behind quills, brushes,
richly-coloured inks, the paraphernalia required
to complete his Gospels, twenty years in the making.

His work captures the times, shines
through the ages on pages of light.

A serious man

from 'Voices in a mystery' collection

The old road's a hard road, little give and lots of take,
when you've a wife with child, a wife who could be your child.
The difference in age mattered; people said I was an old fool
to take on another's pleasure; but when she looked,
radiant, innocent, into this old, seamed face
and took these hands, barklike and scarred
from years of chisel and adze, into hers,
I almost believed her story.
I raised the child as my own.

I was a disappointment to him.
I could never hold a saw's straight line
like I could hold a line of disputation.
I could never release, as he could, the form from wood,
only story and fable from the tangled branches of life.
But until he and I left, at the same time,
me to my desert wilderness, he to his mind's,
he treated me well and fairly;
I called him father and, in his own way,
I think he loved me.

I walked this way once, looking for him,
my wife, red-eyed and weeping, convinced
he'd been taken by men who meant him no good
on his first trip to the city.
Hot, breathless, full of rage and anxiety,
I found the boy. He was with men—
but holding his own in debate and argument against them.
I listened, as the skill and craftsmanship I had never witnessed
in his dealings with wood, came naturally.
There was pride in my chastisement of him.
Now I walk this way again, following the crowd,

looking for the man I lost some years ago,
time close to my heel and fast beating heart.

Through sweat and blood and thorn-gashed pain,
I see a girl with red hair, holding
her mother's hand and watching pensive as we pass,
a girl who once could not stop, who danced and jerked
even in her sleep.
There is a man whose puckered, red and shiny face
radiates calm, his unclouded eyes
free from his devils.
A woman, gravid, content, her gift evident
in belly and smile.
Surrounded by family, the man from the grave,
a grave man, serious, slow, careful,
savouring his new life.
Their silent presence gives witness to grateful thanks;
they live my torment as I lived theirs.
I stumble, hauling this tree,
as rough hewn as if it were my own work,
to the hill, where two women
steadfastly sustain each other against a growing dark.
I thought he may have come;
but I was never truly his,
even though I loved him.

My child bride, as old now and
wrinkled as I was when we first met,
careworn, her worst fear realised,
her son taken by men who would do him harm.
She does not see me,
but would not recognise, in this dried out husk,
the man who supported and loved her all those years,
but who ran away when truth turned to deceit
in his mind.
She turns and I hear the words muttered
to her young companion, held close,

"Unfair, unfair. I have a tomorrow and he has none."
He is near the end;
I have viewed these violations before.
He raises his head one last weary time—
and sees me. He cries out,
"Father, forgive them..."   and he is gone.
I never told him I loved him,
my almost son.

An uncertain light

from 'Voices in a mystery' collection

The old man, steadfast in faith,
strong still, shared bread
and memories with his guests.

"That night.   At supper.   He knew.
His last edict to me—
'Three times. Three times
you will deny me.'
Otherwise, as one of his circle,
I would be taken; without his rock,
what would happen to the foundations?

The others fled, fearful of reprisal.
I didn't blame them.
I felt the need to be near him,
even in the skin of my betrayal.

I think I expected signs,
portents of his power,
quelling of storms, filling of nets,
raising of the dead.
I wanted to see him lash out,
as he had at the temple;
I would have gone to his side,
joined with his fury—no denying.

Instead I shadow-skulked in
courtyard firelight, watching
the night's commotion,
endured looks, whispers,
stern-voiced and nasal—whining speculations,
questions.

I answered,
'No.'   'Not me.'   'Never.'
and then   and then
the cockerel crowed,
raw, tuneless,
summoning an uncertain light."

After his speaking,
the room held a silence
like space between prayers.

IV

On rehearsing "The Birthday Party" by Harold Pinter

she directs

a space
where
nothing has happened
where
anything could happen
a space
waiting to happen
wanting to happen

a pause

a heartbeat of phrases

a
    stab
        of
            words

a pause

a silence
trickles through the text
falls from a drumbeat
a car door slam

a silence

a pause

a space

It's in the nature of birds (to fly)

A busy road in Fulham.
A man walked with a parrot;
unperturbed by clamour,
it journeyed sideways to the
end of the man's shoulder and back,
seesawed gently, cracked open a nut.
The man's wooden leg and eyepatch?
He had neither.

On Putney Bridge, a man stared upriver,
seeing ghosts of rowers, boat races.
He wore a thick, cracked, leather gauntlet;
perched there, a hawk, work, it seemed,
of a skilled taxidermist. Then, some gulls
dived low towards Bishop's Park;
its gold and jet-jewelled eyes
followed them, moved with their every move.
Its claws contracted—a faint wing shrug.
The man stroked the bird, continued his staring.

In St. James' Park the old woman,
smelling of mushrooms and mice, muttered.
She sat on a bench, took
from her stained raincoat pockets
tattered Tesco bags, spilling seed and grain.
In moments, pigeons had settled,
covering her legs, arms, head.
She smiled as she flew to
far-off treetops and turrets.
Some tourists took photographs.

Haunted by a rose

to John Ruskin

Humiliated, terrified from sleep,
spectres from his firelight
on the bedpost,
in his head
as dawn briefly limns
the summits across the lake.

From his tower,
he watches wind driven wavelets
on Coniston Water,
the dun and green
mass of hills,
but sees the stones of Venice;
hears in the air's turbulence
and insistence
the machinery of city
grinding down the human voice.

One voice he hears clearly
above the clamour;
fresh and vivid as her name
and her face in his portrait
of Zipporah downstairs.
Time sharpens her memory
while others of fame
become as unimportant
as his ideas and crusades
in the face of his loss.

The star chamber he made
for children's wonder
showed the sky at his birth;

The conjunctions did not predict
how a rose
would overshadow everything
for the old man of Coniston,
leaving only a truth—
"There is no wealth but life."

Excavation

a handspan, no more,
you would have uncovered
my mystery,
hidden, protected, untouched,
sought by many

a handspan, no more,
my inner depths would have opened
to you, labyrinthine secrets
yielding to hungry eyes,
gentle probings

a handspan to the south
you could have had
a first hint of bounty beyond,
my rich mosaics
my very foundations

a handspan, no more—
instead your barren hieroglyphics note
'test pit 3   70 centimetres
two nails, rusted, north-east corner,
quantity of snail shells'

a handspan, no more,
you would have achieved your desire.

Beams

I

On oak timbers, iron-hardened,
pale-wormed, the building's stories,
told in coded complexities
of purlins, posts, joints
by long-ago craftsmen
with augur and adze.
The report of the house-readers;
careful measurements,
photographs, samples
making sense of messages
obscured by time and usage.

II

The upper-storey frame
has the feel, the keel, the ribs
of a land-locked boat,
built to ride out turbulences
in the roil and current of everyday.

III

In the attic's mote-filled stillness,
blackened beams retain
ancient, smoke-bitter scent,
a ghost of sensation, a link
to those who sailed their lives within.
In pleasantly cluttered rooms below,
the current family's books,
paintings, objects dear and precious,
create a cheerful collage,
a chapter of home and continuity
in the tale of centuries.

Green room

*for Tom and Cecil ***

Carvings on tabletops in the bar
reflect the runes
on Baltic beams upstairs
in the old warehouse;
ciphers recording tallies, cargoes,
hints of ports, voyages
to those who can read
through the marks to the meaning.

A lot of stairs from theatre
to green room and above;
takes puff when you're getting on a bit,
and the centuries hold you back with interest—
mediaeval paving, Georgian brickwork,
pressed boys and men, scrimshaw of Napoleon's finest.

Beams, dreams...

I saw a face.
On pictures.
On the walls of the green room.
A long, northern face,
a history of early mornings,
cold sea frets
in his lines and wrinkles.
A smile of a big, gentle man.
I remembered his slow,
kindly, considered burr,
big hands used to hard graft,
the crafting of words.

*(Tom Hadaway and C.P. Taylor, two playwrights and mentors)

I heard the crash of crates,
haggling for prices,
smelt the diesel and salt
wetness of it all.

More pictures.
Another face. Rounder.
A constant twinkling
behind thick-set glasses;
his Glasgow accent quick,
reflecting his thoughts;
his generosity to actors
as he captured the gold-glints
in the nuggets of their improvisations,
gave them back, polished words on paper;
his late-night tenacity with directors
who watered his script,
used 'widdler' for 'pisser'
in censorshipped days;
his fisherman's ganzies, striped flannel shirts.

When I looked at their photos, yesterday,
I saw men who I had thought old.
They were in their prime.
I had grown old, older than either,
had almost forgotten
they taught me to read
to the meanings
behind their markings,
those younger men who
smiled out at me now.

Bread at E5

Ten met at the table today,
a new communion—the swapping of names,
the talk of scones, goats in Kuala Lumpur,
the meaning of ciabatta—
swirled with the flour dust.

Then I watched as you made the bread
that brought us together;
your hand reached to a soldier's at Waterloo,
the year the leaven was given life,
day by day refreshed,

the mix as simple as faith,
steadfast across the centuries
of a world's turmoil.
We lost ourselves for a while
in the rhythm of a different ferment.

Winter warmer

At the first snow
of this warmer winter,
you say to me,
"I can't sleep. It's ages
since my feet were this cold."
I reply "Put them on mine."
I don't even wince
at the shock of their ice
but lie quietcuddled
as our extremities swap warmths
according to the laws of physics.
Our eyes curtain against
the night's gradual whitening
and I listen to your breathing drift,
slowsoft as snowflakes,
over the day's harsh outlines,
your feet cosy against mine.

At a year's end

Holding hands—or rather
clutching at the reassurance of our fingers,
steadying, familiar, rooted in experience—
we look out for each other, for obstacles in our path,
moving gingerly as one,
senior citizens in a three-legged race.

We witnessed the stumblings of old age
just a short while ago with a sense of
schadenfreude (without the malice, of course).
Overnight, it seems, we now inhabit a reality
of bus seats surrendered to us,
lost words and spectacles.

We briefly envy young ones who,
full of the ease and bound of hares,
overtake our tortoise progress,
eager for the race to midnight,
ready to take on the new year's challenges,
to win the right to become—like us.

You sniff at a sprig of jasmine
exploring the out-of-kilter winter warmth
and your smile tells me
there is flowering still to come.

They talked all night

As sticky-warm as day,
his window open wide
to suck in reluctant cool
from the dark; instead,
the ripple and eddy
of voices, laughter, along
the river valley of back gardens.
He drowned asleep in its murmur,
the night's humidity, sometimes
shaken to the surface
by a harsher cough, a coarser laugh,
a clatter of bottle and glass...

they talked all night once,
on a balcony above the sea,
wrapped in skin to skin love
and a hotel sheet,
the prosecco warm and going flat,
the spiralling of cigarette smoke
chalked against
the sky's blackboard—
the life they planned,
the babies they'd have,
their apple-tree entwined ending...

He's grumbled awake
by the first of the long hauls' landing;
the voices diminish
with the sun's strengthening.
He turns to ask how she slept;
the vast distance of the day stretches
across the empty pillow,
the unfilled space beside him.

V

58°N 137°W

A wilderness sanctuary in Alaska

Glacier Bay—
a glimpse of creation, a cathedral
with a roof of clouds
supported by caryatid mountains,
a floor of ice shards,
reflections;

a place of guillemots and gulls
whispers of otters and humpbacks,
celebrants at an endless sacrament.
The rumbleboom and sharpcrack
of living glaciers' voices
mingle with memories of
long gone First Nation fisherfolk calls,
sailors' saltcroaked shouts,
sheetslap and cablecreak of 'The Discovery,'
to enhance the wilderness silence,
hymn a profound peace
in this place of awe.

Sleeper

from Flying fish in the Bay of Bengal

The very small dog warily eyes
the passers-by with strange clothes,
strange smells. It does not move from
its comfortable, crossed paws position,
but is alert, ready if necessary,
to shake off its torpor and rouse
all friendly souls within earshot
with a voice ten times bigger than its body.

Its mistress lies asleep
on the floor of the verandah,
passed by the same strangers
not three feet away.
Oblivious to the world,
she knows her mouse dog will save her.

Family

from Flying fish in the Bay of Bengal

Look through the window and see the altar
at the heart of the house on the water.
Part of the weave of daily life;
side by side with the television
and favourite chairs.

The ancestors are constant; consulted
on matters of great import or
of little moment. The family
always stays together; those
in spirit and those of the flesh.

The long line of name
and ancestry crosses wars,
poverty, hardship, rejoicing,
governments, emperors and queens.
It is the given on which life is based.

It is the born and yet to be born;
it is the loving and squabbles,
tears and joy. The living altar is
the heartbeat of the home,
everyday present.

Barbados

The next wave took him.

In his youth, through manhood,
he had been vigorous, strong,
a swimmer against the tide,
the man who went further, deeper,
confident in his ability
to reach any shore.

Old age had rendered him gaunt,
its current stripping muscle, piece
by unrewarded piece. Now he stood,
waist deep in breakers on a Caribbean beach,
a coral sculpture made unsteady
by hammer blows of surf.

Other swimmers, enjoying their prime,
delighting in boisterous cross-currents,
silver-glinted foam, scarcely noticed
the old man in shorts,
too big for skeletal legs,
slip under.

Dürnstein

A castle on the Danube where Richard I was held hostage

Perhaps the hawk,
craghovering over Dürnstein,
hunts the trace of a song
that Blondel left behind

or searches along the Danube banks for
maidens snatched by the River King,
treasures drowned, plagues and monasteries,
dynasties made
and disappeared;

or listens for the music of the river's moods
in Strauss' panegyric,
the ripples and rills of Liszt,
the heart's delight of Lehar,
Wagner's sturm und drang,
Mozart's infinite variety—
liquid hauntings of notes, voices...

or waits for the river's traffic to pass,
then plummets through history, fable and tune
to earth and the unsuspecting meal.

Havana – two snapshots

I

A once-elegant lady, bones
prominent under delicate, thinning skin.

The city's buildings wear their age
like Giacometti sculptures,
skeletons tricked out with fragments
from earlier times, dying from
salt, humidity, metal fatigue.

Through empty window frames, you can see
rooms rot inside, stained, puddled, empty of life.

Cradled by decay, supported from collapse
by wooden beams, verandah railings
on the second floor, draped with hand-done laundry;
a man, bare chested, lifts his child
over the washing to see the bustle below.

II

A young woman at a bus stop.
She shares her wait with forty others.

It has been an hour and twenty minutes
since the last bus; no-one knows
when the next will arrive.
No time has been wasted; she has
met a friend of her mother's whom she calls 'Aunty,'

swapped recipes, flirted gently
with two boys, made a date to meet
one of them; the bus arrives, full.
They sardine on, breath and bodies
melting into one another.

They have learnt to accept since fifty-nine,
looking for good things in everyday obstacles,
knowing the world outside moves on,
resigning themselves to limited choices,
patient in their imposed time bubble.

In the near-empty Square of the Revolution,
overlooked by Ministries, vultures,
an image of Che,
it's hard to imagine the throng summoned
to hear Fidel's seven hour speech.

Two million of them waited,
listened with rum and resignation.

Estuary walk in mist

Sometimes the sea
in strength and perversity
breaches dune walls,
sweeps on to embrace
estuary wetness
nervous of the merging.

The short lived passion of waters
floods plants, paths,
unwary creatures;
the drawback uncovers
a transformed landscape,
a mingle of sea and land detritus...

scraps of seaweed flap
from ripped branches,
washing drooped in the rain;
bleachwood sculptures
of gnarled hands, women dancing;
the carcass of a sheep

picked and pecked,
torn and riven
by gull, crow, raven;
stark ribs
a carrion place
like the river's dead staithes.

The waves have violated
the negotiated embrace of the margins.
A sea fret laments,
weeps a veil over the transgression.

Storm

Black backed gulls with killer eyes
Hover over churning sea,
Steal the drowning men's last cries.

What final thought with each one lies
Looking heavenward to see
Black backed gulls with killer eyes?

Savage waters claim their prize,
Salt waves turn the final key,
Steal the drowning men's last cries.

Winged aloft on thermals' rise,
Bird and soul as one set free,
Black backed gulls with killer eyes.

Rising winds capture their sighs,
Add them to the storm's decree,
Steal the drowning men's last cries.

So it is when each one dies,
Never knowing what could be—
Black backed gulls with killer eyes
Steal the drowning men's last cries.

Fly

Wing tips ink-dipped
kittiwakes reel raucous
over Quayside streets,
snow-downed tarrocks*
safe, nested
on the Bridge's sheer cliff ledges.

They look down on forgotten chares,
secret Georgian squares,
half-timbered merchant houses,
steep streets, arches,
Norman keep, Dog Leap Stairs
enduring beyond the 'party city.'

They note how ebb and flow
swirl the banks like
Vincent's brush strokes
on each bend and curve
the river of war
the river of fish.

Ghosts of cranes
Fish Quay crates
ravaged Priory
Black Middens' treachery—
they meet with others from Staple Island,
take on the pelagic journey
to unseen winter seas;
with spring breezes of promise,
they make their return.

I once flew the Tyne—
I feel shifting winds
point me home.

* Tarrock – a fisherman's word for a young kittiwake

Estuary

The runriver of evening tide
in soft, steady copperplate;
the cursive of waves;
the jottings of terns
in their diving hunt;
criss cross runes of cormorant staithes;
the rhyme and rhythm of language unspoken.
Time holds the heron watchful,
glanced by waning gold,
a punctuation on ripple and burnish,
still, in the familiar strangeness
written in a twice a day tale.

Hauxley in Doggerland I

Around 6100 BC a twenty-one metre high tsunami, caused by the underwater Storegga slide, just off Norway, struck the east coast of Scotland. The area known as Doggerland, a low lying land bridge of the best hunting and fowling in Europe, connecting the east coast of England and Denmark, was inundated by the tsunami and became the North Sea.

The trees of Hauxley, a beach in Northumberland, were exposed by rising sea levels cutting back the sand dunes. Fossilised human footprints have also been discovered here.

The hunter pauses
behind the tree, breathing hard
after a long search.

He sees, on rough bark,
ants processing to their nest,
bearing leaf fragments.

Near him he notes trees
full of ripening nuts, ready
to stock winter stores.

A butterfly lands,
nervous, on a twig; squirrels
'chuck' from tall branches.

The hunter settles, waits;
the forest calms around him;
he and it are one.

The quarry's rank scent,
carried on the forest breeze,
signals its closeness.

In a rage of grunts,
the red-eyed boar, fearsome tusked,
scatters undergrowth.

His bristles quiver;
at his snort, his sounder* root
into the clearing.

The hunter too quivers;
alert to the kill, he picks
the nearest young boar.

He takes a deep breath,
readies his fire-sharpened spear,
signals the others.

Two scatter the group
with rocks and shouts; the hunter
strikes. Blood. The hunt done.

The forest quiets,
anticipating the roar
of tsunami tide.

Below the dunes, exposed,
a dark line along the beach
marks forest remains.

Eight thousand years old,
alchemically altered
roots and stumps appear

as fabled creatures,
hybrids of wood, stone, rising
from their bed of peat.

* sounder—a group of boar

I touch a tree, place
a finger on the dark soil,
where a hunter's bones

may lie, waiting for
tide and time to discover,
like footprints once found

at Hauxley. For now,
earth on both our hands creates
a handshake across time.

Hauxley in Doggerland II

a footprint
laid bare
by harsh tides
scouring sand

a hunter's footprint
laid down in peat
as he stalked
wild boar, auroch
in wet woodland fringes
left by fracture
and tsunami

a step across time

the press of my foot
lingering in the wet sand
dissolves as I watch

dissolves as I

dissolv

d

.

Before I go

Come with me to the beach at Hauxley,
April morning, cloudless blue,
barely a breeze but a nip and tang in the air—
made for walking, following
paths of sprinkled coal, oystercatchers and turnstones
brief flights ahead at the tide's incoming edge
splashes of foam
sea diamonds in sun sparkle,
a soothing discourse of non-stop waves,
Coquet Island white, watchful.

Come with me there, so we can seek
the tracks of waders lightly patterned,
holes in damp sand marking hunting pauses;
so I can pick a treasure of sea glass
opaqued and smoothly rounded
to add to your collection;
so I can watch your face,
grown lovelier over years,
look out to the horizon,
relax with memories.

On Hauxley Beach

The wind drops.
The sea turns.
Choppy, insistent,
it hustles feeding
oyster catchers
turnstones, redshanks,
up the rock and seaweed canyons
to the worm cast and wave rippled beach

where

this January morning
few venture—
walkers of dogs
walkers of long distance walks
walkers-off of the season's excesses;
a horse, in need of grooming,
plods past
two strollers on the shore

who pause to see,

backlit by lazy sun,
a skyline of oystershell hues,
silhouettes of
a power station
towers
wind turbines,
ten thousand or more
Fitbit steps distant;
a Don Quixote landscape
an imagining away.

In a dreaming

(Allendale, Northumberland)

Native Australians' narrative maps are painted with the range of pigments available. They dream and sing the history of the land, which belongs to no-one.

The terrain, a map
on green grounding, picked out in
dun brown, plumb grey, silver glint.

Peewit flock to ploughing—
Vincent's birds, daubed on fields,
crow away from second plantings.

Tracking through bushes,
roe bucks trail
soft calls of hidden does.

On stone wall thruffs,
rabbit and mouse
keep their watchful distance.

The windhover faces
into its element,
dives for bankside voles.

Hints of falling rills
drizzle the silence in the folds, rolls,
scars of deserted hills.

In its dales and dead tunnels,
under paling skies, rib cages of cloud,
the land of lead, lime and lapwing dreams.

Before the mowing

Sheepspin clouds
tease the hilltops,
the far Cheviots ancient
landfold miles away.

On the curlew high meadows
pollened with tormentil,
trefoil, vetch,
bruised with cornflower, self heal,

white-tailed bees bumble,
harvesting, full and fat,
heath bees buzz and hover,
map a zig zag to the nest.

Sheltered in the conversation
between wind and rowan,
I watch an afternoon's lifetime
span across Allen's valley.

On seeing the cairn for two shepherds

(for Jock Scott, Willie Middlemass)

I

Simple facts. 17th. November 1962.
Two shepherds, friends,
perished in the snow.

The stern-inscribed stone,
secure in its space;
a telling presence.

Lichen circles encroach
the base, the chiselling,
the first T of SCOTT,
above the N of NATIONAL;
the S of SNOW is beginning
to vanish, melting;
the place is clothing the cairn,
slowly, inexorably,
shaping it to the rugged curves
of the surrounding hills.

Twigs of civilization
among tussocks of wind-whipped spart grass,
gather near the ill-kept road;
wood carved signposts,
'Public footpath to Biddlestone 2 ¾'
'Ewartly Shank ½;'
fingers to a distant nowhere.
Fence posts umbilically linked by wire,
a snow post, rusted white red black-
spelks of humanity
in the flesh of a hard land
which claims its own,
gives them final comfort.

II

By the church, early swallows
wheel chase climb let,
look to repair last year's nests;
wood sorrel primrose violets
blossom in burgeoning woods.

Here on the high ground
far up the climbing switchback
potholed old man's elbow
of singletrack,
it's bone-cold on a warm April day.

Not easy land; a place to love
yet fear its isolate beauty;
its tracks wind, turn,
disappear into little-known places,
cattle-hiding valleys.

From the fragile safety of the sheep path
summitting a steep, pot-pie hill,
wind-whipped lambs and ewes
nestle close, watch, still,
as we, bent to the blast, reach the cairn, see

subdued in the kraal of laws and knowes,
a small group of farm buildings,
diminished by their singular setting,
half an uncrossed mile away,
as distant as lost lives.

Two days at Catton

Day 1

Autumn winds raid the valley early
in a wild circling from a colder place.
Sturdy dry-stone walls are suddenly fragile,
offer no lee to plants
flattened, horizontal and shaking,
while meres of grass ripple, race,
break round the white reefs of sheep.
Along the steep hairpin road, rowan,
shocking red, hints at other fruits to come;
a sudden drop reveals
a stand of pines, tussling
like corralled beasts; one weak giant
at the herd's edge has fallen
to predator gusts and panic
spreads to the branches of the others.

Low, lowering, clouds sprint and spread,
gusting rain, bringing with them
a too-early dark,
a changing promise.

Day 2

In the late summer sunshine,
sykes vein the valley
towards the artery of the Allen.
Rooted in the land, four-square and sightless,
deserted families ago, buildings
wait out the remainder
of their empty-room existence,
stones warming in pointless anticipation.
Hearted in the walls,
a bustle of ponies, trains, lead-carrying
to the Tyne, tracks and people

networking the strung-out dwellings.
A palpable silence, calming,
terrifying in the hills' folds;
hikers portering their rucksacks
replace the souls who passed here;
the harsh weather of yesterday
gives way to gentler skies.

Blawearie

I

The wind's at our backs;
October wind, cool with
winter's approaching promise, a hint
of bleak, sere times ahead.

The sun plays chase
with veils of rain,
blue skies teasing
like the year so far.

Mud clings us to earth
as we trudge up the track,
but as we pause to catch breath,
to take a nourishment
from glimpses of
distant slumbered hills,
for a wing beat, we hover
like the buzzards overhead,
gifted a view of ages,
an ever-changing permanence.

II

Here, in a criss crossed landscape
of track and trail,
traces in stone of lives lived remote,
deaths honoured,
testaments in massive rock
or crafted walls.

Open to the skies, the vagaries of weather,
they offer, to travellers' curiosity,
intimate glimpses of existence
in a fabled landscape.

Ancestors hewn
from the same birth quarry,
virgin mossed and lichened, these relics,
the space of millennia between them,
are spanned by a rainbow promise,
linked by the paths of people and beasts.

Cubbing on Lowes Fell

Trees strip back,
reveal the muscle
of a landscape
honed by toil and time.

Across a tussocked field,
hard by the sinew of dry-stone wall,
a dozen or so riders
on sturdy hunters; farmers
who live the land in their everyday,
not the posh-pink of hunting prints.

They gather, catch up on harvests,
early signs of winter, while
rough-coated hounds cast around,
reading the air and damp grass.

The horn's double note clarions,
scatters the last of the mist,
regiments the riders,
calls the pack to order.

Guided by scent,
each others' familiarity,
the hunt sets off down
the almost invisible vein
of ancient greenpath,
disappears behind
arteries of hedges,
fades into seasons,
rhythms of landscape,
masters and servants in turn,
a shire's pulse and impulse.

VI

A passing – Nine cantos

Canto I Acts of duty and love

Each stamp in her book
a reluctant Sunday School attended
in the damp, evercold chapel
where God sees all–
those in peril on the sea,
in fathomed dark beneath.
Organ wheeze and tuneless hymning
drowned the ceaseless waves' intoning,
plainsong over deep seam staves
below the restless bay.

"Jesus washing the disciples' feet"–
a favourite, reminder of her dad
in the tin bath on the clippie mat,
fire blazing, mottling her face and legs,
scrubbing the knots and knuckles of his spine,
his back a tattooed map of coal splinters;
released by the flannel,
the man emerged from his daily baptism in
scummed cooling water,
a ritual, a welcome home,
a keeping safe.

Canto II March – a return to cold

We talked a little of weather,
the unseasonality of it,
how it was this time last year
when drought was mentioned,
how we thought the country unprepared
for that contingency and what
faced us now under leaden skies,
cutting winds, disproportionate snowdrifts.

We had considered the conversation over;
her mother, full after Sunday lunch,
warm and cushioned, seemed to doze,
mouth slightly open, eyes shut,
gaining innocence and losing wrinkles
as she relaxed.
We reached for the papers,
glad of some private time.

"...and another thing," said the old lady,
unexpectedly. "That bed's too big for me
in this weather. Stretch out with your foot
and it's freezing." She paused. Sighed.
"When I reach my arm across
to the other side, there's
no-one warm to hold.
I feel the cold much more, now."

Canto III Cambois

In the river of her speech,
the loops, the diversions,
words like leaves
Armada'd on the waters.

She spoke of her father
   who trimmed coals
in lung coating darkness
   of North Sea colliers
stoked-ready, eager for London;
   who shared the shed
next the Seven Stars with
   hard-muscled men,
blue scarred, gentle
   in her pig-tailed presence.

She told of her grandfather,
   a Northern billiards champion,
his proud, cue'd portrait
   hanging still in the Institute,
though his silver bowl
   and status were lost
to the unforgiving hunger
   of the Miners' Strike.

She recited the Rows
   like the telling of a rosary—
Store, Sinker, Chapel, Union—
   the gossip behind each
unlocked door, each 'double raa;'
   firelight vigils with
her granny, stiff-backed,
   whose clouded eyes and clear mind
reached back to veiled,
   black gowned earlier days.

In the hospital room, her voice
slowed, pooled round the story
of Geordie's ducks' mysterious end;
eyes closing, she slept away her decades.

Canto IV Kings Mill

On the clock
the second hand jerks
clicks the morning away
from the five a.m. shock
past a missed breakfast
towards hollowbellied noon.

Porters have wheeled you
through long, deserted,
Saturday-afternoon corridors,

a mediaeval effigy
on a hospital bed,
from A&E to x-ray x-ray to A&E

back and forth like the questions
name? date of birth?
how old? what year?
which monarch? where do you live?
heard, answered with varying
degrees of volume and certainty

while in the spaces between
blood samples   blood pressure
temperature   saline drips   bed pan
your daughter recites
a well-rehearsed litany
of your falls and illnesses

to a bewilderment of short sleeves
navy blue light blue
eau de nil white mauve
who register information
with 'Ah bless'
and serious eyes.

Mapped on the monitor
your heart beat blips
graphs its way through the hours.

Canto V Sleeps with dinosaurs

I lay under its bones—
cold, stiff, breathing in
night breaths of a hundred others.
In the great hall,
their sleep music
lulled me not at all.

Body-restless,
my mind wilded outside
with the season's first storms.
Turbulent winds and phone calls away,
you struggled with
a tempest of feelings.

Walking drowned pavements,
early morning Sunday,
brought a brief breathing space
before the next unstoppable.
It was enough; I had seen clues
in the skeletons of dinosaurs.

Canto VI Serenissima

A grand old lady with sea-stained skirt,
she displays her jewels, wears
the signs of her age with pride.
She retains beauty enough
to give breath a pause
to attract second glances
her beguiling conversations
stretch across centuries of topics,
her tide-rhythmed moods
intrigue poets, painters;
lovers come to her for blessing,
wise folk to decipher allegories
on panels and murals,
wanderers reflect on her bridges
and pilgrims seek comfort
in prayer-and-incense filled churches.

Strolling that morning
we were part of the city;
the *caliga* swirling from the lagoon,
fur-swathed women with

groomed and pampered dogs,
elegant couples in each *campo's* festive market,
gondola passengers wrapped against December-chill.
We looked along arm-stretch wide *calli*,
made for whispers and secrets;
at quiet, cramped *canalli*, the tide
lapping at damp-ravaged
doorways of once grand houses;
in tiny shops of masks,
Venetian paper, Murano bracelets;
through windows of larger shops,
discreet in designer elegance.

The city charmed;
we reached for each other's hand,
for no reason, on the bridge
across the Grand Canal.

The phone call came.

Canto VII A mortality of days

At this time of day,
at this time of year,
there is a frail and fading
delicacy about the light,
permeating Bewick etched trees,
the cauled remains of leaves,
in their long, stark sleep
before a wakening.

Grey's curfew bell
calls in the early dark;
a chorister's clear voice
soars Rosetti's opening line
to midwintered rafters; for some,
who suffer unseasonable loss,

there is a bleak beauty of solace
in a long-ago birth.

Canto VIII After

The day after your funeral
Was one of stillness,
flawless in its sky
searing in its cold.
For the first time in a very long time,
we didn't have to plan you
into any activities.
We did nothing without guilt.

So that day, we did nothing.
Without guilt.

Canto IX For a moment

The churchyard still, bone-chilled,
windless, a Wedgewood scene
of frost and clear morning sky.
Two tableau'd figures,
stick-puppet silhouettes,
motionless as the day.
They hear our gravelled steps;
one raises his arm
in greeting, benediction.

There is a hole,
surprisingly deep for
such a small casket;
some soil next to it,
more covered with
green waterproof,
humped like the beginnings
of a Sunday School project—

"There is a green hill far away..."
The casket, light oak,
has her name, engraved
on a brass plate;
the stone, too, amended
so her name is joined to his,
as in life, by 'Always loved.'
The vicar, a warm, humane
handshake of a man, begins
to recite words of comfort.

The church clock bells once,
pure, almost shocking
in the clear air,
then punctuates the reading
with calm, measured,
ten o'clock notes.
A blackbird flutes
to himself in the bushes,
scuttles through a leaf pile.

A voice, a song, a bell
weave for a moment
a garment of hope and promise;
the casket is lowered easily
in its cradle of black ribbons
into its waiting rest;
a fragile ice of silence returns
to sharpen a sound,
the handful of soil-scatter on wood.

A pause.
A moment taken out of time.
A reflection.
Then the earth moves again—
through frosted stubble,
green shoots strain for sky

as we strive for light,
some way to make sense
of the infinite about us.

The sun has become warmer.
We are alive. Holding hands,
we walk towards the rest of our day.

A garden at the end of the world

Evening, warm scented
lemon, almond, myrtle
extending the day's fragrance,
sunshine heat trapped in leaf and fruit,
released into moth-flitting dusk.

Perched on the water bowl
doves took sips before roosting;
a nightingale began its 'hoo-eet' call,
betraying its presence in the rose bush
staked on the southern wall.

The garden; at ease with friends;
work put behind;
wine-breath'd conversation
stimulating, righting perceived wrongs,
taking the measure of a good life.

The guests left, the host extinguished the torches,
crushed and smelled rosemary, to ease his head.
Above the cypress,
the stencilled hulk of mountain loomed,
late summer thunder trespassed the garden's peace.

In the night, the wind picked up,
thrashing umbrella pines, melding
their sounds to the nearby sea's.
A boy looked from his window,
watched the water in the pool fracture, tremble.

Dawn. The gardener came to dig, prune, pick
fruit or vegetables for the pot.
Stretching, soothing a backache sixty years old,
he felt newly-raked sod shift;
looking up, he noticed smoke from the peak.

By mid-day, he could no longer see or work;
his master told him to find his family, stay with them;
by afternoon, grey-snow blizzard of ash and pumice
covered plants, benches, tools, filled in
the breathing holes of terra cotta pots.

No birds sang;
no clever words;
no flow of water or wine;
no drift of lavender;
a bitter odour of burning.

Preserved in the frescoes of Pompeii,
the garden lived on in memories
under the depth of debris and centuries.

Coda

Gulls no limits know,
nor winds, nor tides; set free,
a soul may join them.